S0-AVK-223

Mi pez = My fish
3305233196660
jlks   8/31/15

MI PEZ
MY FISH

Norman D. Graubart
Traducción al español: Christina Green

PowerKiDS
press™
New York

Published in 2014 by The Rosen Publishing Group, Inc.
29 East 21st Street, New York, NY 10010

Copyright © 2014 by The Rosen Publishing Group, Inc.

All rights reserved. No part of this book may be reproduced in any form without permission in writing from the publisher, except by a reviewer.

First Edition

Book Design: Colleen Bialecki
Photo Research: Katie Stryker   Traducción al español: Christina Green

Photo Credits: Cover weechia@ms11.url.com.tw/flickr/Getty Images; p. 5 Vlad61/Shutterstock.com; p. 7 iStockphoto/Thinkstock; p. 9 Vangert/Shutterstock.com; pp. 11, 17 bluehand/Shutterstock.com; p. 13 Beth Swanson/Shutterstock.com; p. 15 illuta goean/Shutterstock.com; p. 19 Arie v.d. Wolde/Shutterstock.com; p. 21 KidStock/Blend Images/Getty Images; p. 23 MattJones/Shutterstock.com.

Library of Congress Cataloging-in-Publication Data

Graubart, Norman D.
 My fish = Mi pez / by Norman D. Graubart ; translated by Christina Green. — First edition.
    pages cm. — (Pets are awesome! = ¡Las mascotas son geniales!)
English and Spanish.
Includes index.
ISBN 978-1-4777-3307-3 (library)
1. Aquarium fishes—Juvenile literature. 2. Fishes—Juvenile literature. I. Green, Christina, translator. II. Graubart, Norman D. My fish. III. Graubart, Norman D. My fish. Spanish. IV. Title. V. Title: Mi pez.
SF457.25G7318 2014
639.34—dc23
                         2013022456

Web Sites: Due to the changing nature of Internet links, PowerKids Press has developed an online list of Web sites related to the subject of this book. This site is updated regularly. Please use this link to access the list:
www.powerkidslinks.com/paa/fish/
Manufactured in the United States of America

CPSIA Compliance Information: Batch # W14PK3: For Further Information contact Rosen Publishing, New York, New York at 1-800-237-9932

CONTENIDO

CONTENTS

Los peces son mascotas coloridas.

_____

Fish are colorful pets.

4

5

A un grupo de peces se le llama **banco**.

A group of fish is called a **school**.

7

Todos los peces respiran debajo del agua usando sus **branquias**.

All fish breathe underwater using their **gills**.

Uno de los peces más populares es la carpa dorada, o *goldfish*.
Este pez proviene originalmente de China.

One of the most popular pet fish is the goldfish. Goldfish originally came from China.

Todos los peces globo tienen cuatro dientes.
Usan sus fuertes dientes para triturar moluscos.

All puffer fish have four teeth. They use their strong teeth to crush shellfish.

13

La **pintarroja ocelada** es un pequeño tiburón y es la mascota más común entre los tiburones. En la naturaleza, vive en las costas de Australia.

Epaulette sharks are some of the most common pet sharks. In the wild, they live only off the coast of Australia.

14

Al pez betta le gusta estar solo en su tanque.

_____

Bettas like to be alone in their tanks.

En la naturaleza, el pez arcoíris se encuentra sólo en un lago de Indonesia.

In the wild, the Boeseman's rainbowfish is found only in a single lake in Indonesia.

19

Alimentar a tu pez puede
ser divertido.

Feeding your fish can be fun.

Si cuidas bien tu pecera, se verá hermosa.

_____

If you take care of your fish tank, it will look beautiful.

23

PALABRAS QUE DEBES SABER
WORDS TO KNOW

(la) pintarroja ocelada
epaulette shark

(las) branquias
gills

(el) banco
school

ÍNDICE

INDEX